Hunting
the
Dinosaurs
and Other Prehistoric Animals

For a free color catalog describing Gareth Stevens's list of high-quality books, call 1-800-341-3569 (USA) or 1-800-461-9120 (Canada).

The editors gratefully thank Claudia Berghaus, Diane Gabriel, and the Geology Section of the Milwaukee Public Museum, Milwaukee, Wisconsin, for their enthusiastic cooperation and technical assistance; Rich Krueger, Dinosaur State Park, Rocky Hill, Connecticut; and a special thanks to Matthew Peterson of Milwaukee, Wisconsin, for his invaluable assistance.

Library of Congress Cataloging-in-Publication Data

Dixon, Dougal.
    Hunting the Dinosaurs
    (The New dinosaur library)
    "First published in The age of dinosaurs: a photographic record"—T.p. verso.
    Includes index.
    Summary: Examines how paleontologists discover, study, classify, reconstruct, and restore the fossil remains of many kinds of dinosaurs.
1. Dinosaurs—Juvenile literature. [1. Paleontology. 2. Dinosaurs. 3. Fossils] I. Burton, Jane, ill. II. Kirk, Steve, ill. III. Title. IV. Series: Dixon, Dougal. New dinosaur library.
QE862.D5D54 1987   567.9'1   87-6461
ISBN 1-55532-284-0
ISBN 1-55532-259-X (lib. bdg.)

This North American edition first published in 1987 by

Gareth Stevens Publishing
1555 North RiverCenter Drive, Suite 201
Milwaukee, Wisconsin 53212, USA

This U.S. edition © 1987. Based on *The Age of Dinosaurs*, by Jane Burton and Dougal Dixon, conceived and produced by Eddison/Sadd Editions, London, and first published in the United Kingdom and Australia by Sphere Books, London, 1984, and in the United States of America, under the title *Time Exposure*, by Beaufort Books, New York, 1984.

This format © 1987 by Gareth Stevens, Inc.
Artwork illustrations © Eddison/Sadd Editions, 1984.
Photographs on cover and page 23 © Jane Burton/Bruce Coleman 1984.
Photographs on page 22 courtesy of Milwaukee Public Museum.
Any additional material and illustrations © 1987 by Gareth Stevens, Inc.

Design: Laurie Shock.
Background photography in selected photos: Norman Tomalin, Paul Wakefield, David Houston.
Photo retouching: Kay Robinson.
Line drawing on page 18 (top): Andrew Farmer.
Line drawing on page 18 (center) reproduced courtesy ofBritish Museum (Natural History).
Additional text: MaryLee Knowlton.
Series editors: MaryLee Knowlton and Mark Sachner.

Technical consultant: Diane Gabriel, Assistant Curator of Paleontology, Milwaukee Public Museum

Printed in the United States of America

6 7 8 9 10 11 12 98 97 96 95 94 93

At this time, Gareth Stevens, Inc., does not use 100 percent recycled paper, although the paper used in our books does contain about 30 percent recycled fiber. This decision was made after a careful study of current recycling procedures revealed their dubious environmental benefits. We will continue to explore recycling options.

Hunting
the
Dinosaurs
and Other Prehistoric Animals

Photography by
Jane Burton

Text by
Dougal Dixon

Artwork by Alan Male & Steve Kirk

Gareth Stevens Publishing
Milwaukee

Hunting
the
Dinosaurs
and Other Prehistoric Animals

The
First
Dinosaurs

The
Jurassic
Dinosaurs

The
Last
Dinosaurs

Hunting the Dinosaurs
and Other Prehistoric Animals

Looking at a skeleton or the fossilized remains of a prehistoric animal is an exciting experience. It makes us wonder about many things: What did the animal actually look like? What kinds of sounds did it make? What was the Earth like millions of years ago, when that animal roamed the land, swam the seas, or sailed the skies? How are animals of today related to prehistoric beasts? And why did that animal, and others like it, die out millions of years before the first humans appeared on the Earth?

This book is about these and many other questions. It is about our Earth and the animals that lived here millions of years ago. It is also about how scientists study prehistoric Earth and fossil life forms, and about how they reconstruct and restore the remains of many thousands of extinct animals.

CONTENTS

Introduction...6
The Changing Earth...6
Plant Life on the Earth..8
Animal Life on the Earth...10
Classifying the Reptiles..12
Running and Flying...14
Swimming and Burrowing..16
Scientists Study the Dinosaurs...18
Reconstructions and Restorations....................................20
A Museum Restoration..22
A Photographic Restoration...23
The Discoveries...24

Fun Facts About Dinosaurs..28
More Books About Dinosaurs...29
Where to See the Dinosaurs..29
New Words..30
Index and Pronunciation Guide...32

INTRODUCTION

Have you ever seen a skeleton of a dinosaur? Did you wonder what the dinosaur looked like when it was alive?

Paleontologists are scientists who study the remains of animals no longer alive. These remains are called *fossils*. Fossils are all the evidence that we have of some animals that no longer live on Earth. These animals are *extinct*.

The ages of prehistoric animals go back to hundreds of millions of years ago. The Age of Dinosaurs goes back to 225 million years ago. For 140 million years the dinosaurs ruled the Earth. Sixty-five million years ago, they became extinct.

THE CHANGING EARTH

The hills and mountains of the Earth seem very old to us. The youngest mountain chain is the Himalayas.

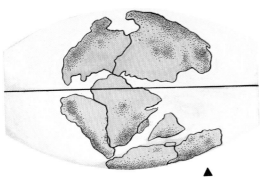

180 million years ago, the continents were all joined. In the north was Laurasia. In the south was Gondwanaland.

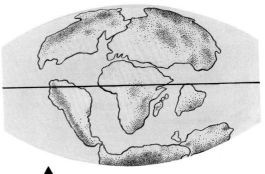

During the time of the dinosaurs, the continents began to split up.

They are only 50 million years old. But the Earth is much older than that — 4,600 million years old.

Other features of the Earth are young if we think in Earth-age terms. Rivers, lakes, forests and deserts have all changed. Even the *continents* have changed their shapes and locations.

The continents are huge rafts of rock that float over the surface of the Earth. They move because of shifts deep below the surface.

The study of the history of the Earth is called *paleogeography*. Paleogeographers study rocks to find out the way the Earth looked in times past.

The coastlines, mountains, and ▶ inland seas were in different places, too. The blue and white on this map show where water and land were in Jurassic North America.

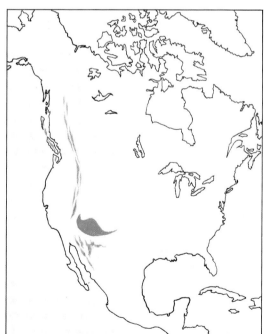

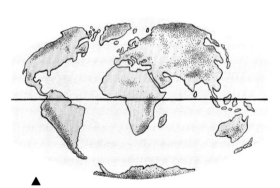

▲
They are still moving — a few inches (centimeters) a year.

PLANT LIFE ON THE EARTH

Like animals, plants also become *fossilized*. The study of plant fossils is called *paleobotany*.

Plants make their own food from water and minerals from the soil. This food is used by the plant and by animals that eat it. So the types of animals that live in an area depend on the types of plants that grow there.

Different types of plants grow in different parts of the world.

Over millions of years plants *evolved* from single cells. They developed leaves and stems. Great forests evolved.

These are psilophytes, one of the earliest groups of plants. They were knee-high. They lived on river banks in Scotland.

The first forests were ferns and horsetails. Some were 100 ft (30 m) high. These forests evolved into *coniferous* forests. Later, flowering plants evolved. Last came grasses — only 50 million years ago.

As the plant life on Earth changed, so did animals. Some *adapted*, and some became extinct.

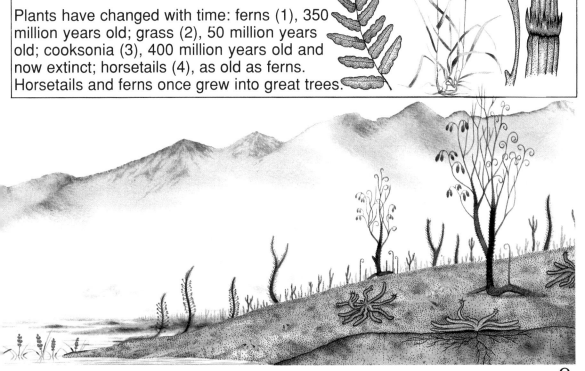

Plants have changed with time: ferns (1), 350 million years old; grass (2), 50 million years old; cooksonia (3), 400 million years old and now extinct; horsetails (4), as old as ferns. Horsetails and ferns once grew into great trees.

ANIMAL LIFE ON THE EARTH

The first animals were single cells. They moved about in the seas, eating single-celled plants. Slowly they evolved into many-celled animals. Some developed backbones. They are called *vertebrates*. The first fish to leave the water were freshwater fish. They were stranded on land when their lakes dried up. They developed lungs to breathe and sturdy fins to move themselves to another pond. Soon the *amphibians* developed. They could move about on land. But they still had to return to the pond to lay their eggs.

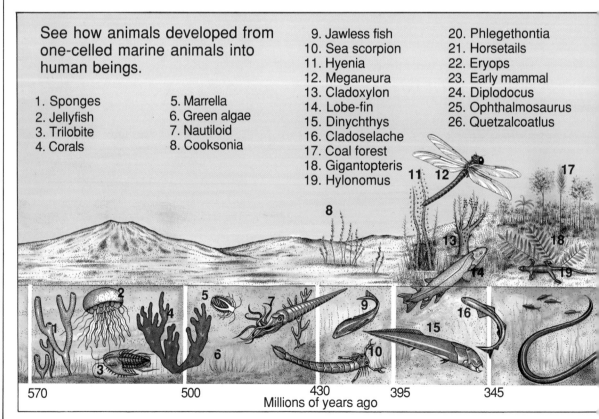

See how animals developed from one-celled marine animals into human beings.

1. Sponges
2. Jellyfish
3. Trilobite
4. Corals
5. Marrella
6. Green algae
7. Nautiloid
8. Cooksonia
9. Jawless fish
10. Sea scorpion
11. Hyenia
12. Meganeura
13. Cladoxylon
14. Lobe-fin
15. Dinychthys
16. Cladoselache
17. Coal forest
18. Gigantopteris
19. Hylonomus
20. Phlegethontia
21. Horsetails
22. Eryops
23. Early mammal
24. Diplodocus
25. Ophthalmosaurus
26. Quetzalcoatlus

570   500   430   395   345
Millions of years ago

Reptiles were the next step in *colonizing* the land. They could breathe air and walk on land. They did not have to return to the water to lay eggs because they laid hard-shelled eggs. One group of reptiles became *mammal-like*. They died out, but first they gave rise to mammals. The mammals were small. They were not important at that time.

The tiny mammals appeared during the Age of Dinosaurs. They changed little in 130 million years. The dinosaurs ruled the Earth for 140 million years. Then they died out and mammals took over. Humans have been here only between two and five million years.

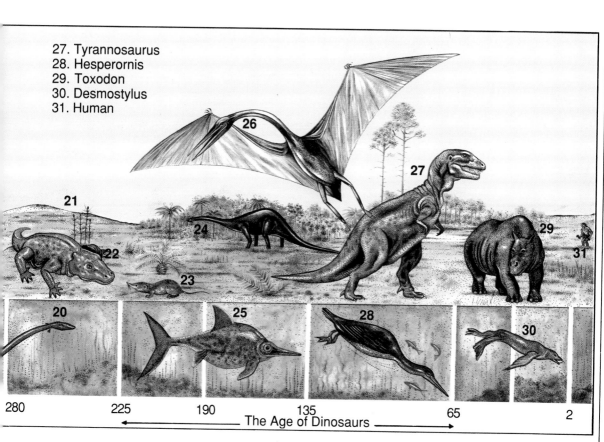

27. Tyrannosaurus
28. Hesperornis
29. Toxodon
30. Desmostylus
31. Human

280   225   190   135   65   2
The Age of Dinosaurs

CLASSIFYING THE REPTILES

A reptile is an animal that lays its eggs on land. It has no internal, or inner, way to control its body temperature. So it is called *"cold-blooded."* It has a scaly or horny skin.

Today's reptiles include these animals: snakes, lizards, crocodiles, alligators, tortoises, turtles, and New Zealand's tuatara. Reptiles do not play as big a role in the animal world today as in the past. They once ruled the Earth.

Many people mistakenly call all prehistoric reptiles dinosaurs. Many prehistoric reptiles did not even live during the Age of Dinosaurs. Dinosaurs belong to a group of reptiles called archosaurs. Dinosaurs are divided into two types of archosaurs: Saurischia, or "lizard-hipped" dinosaurs, and Ornithischia, or "bird-hipped" dinosaurs.

Euparkeria was the kind of thecodont that evolved into the dinosaurs.

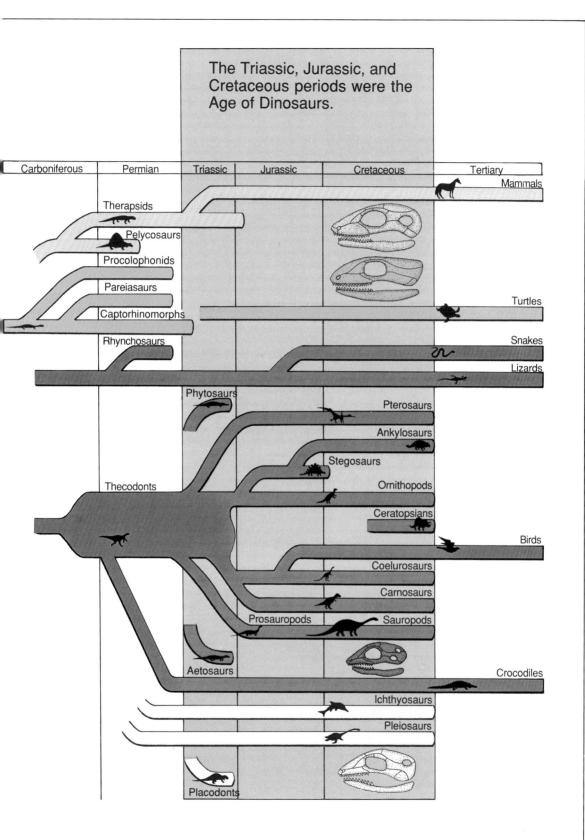

The Triassic, Jurassic, and Cretaceous periods were the Age of Dinosaurs.

| Carboniferous | Permian | Triassic | Jurassic | Cretaceous | Tertiary |

Mammals

Therapsids

Pelycosaurs

Procolophonids

Pareiasaurs

Captorhinomorphs

Turtles

Rhynchosaurs

Snakes

Lizards

Phytosaurs

Pterosaurs

Ankylosaurs

Stegosaurs

Thecodonts

Ornithopods

Ceratopsians

Birds

Coelurosaurs

Carnosaurs

Prosauropods

Sauropods

Aetosaurs

Crocodiles

Ichthyosaurs

Pleiosaurs

Placodonts

13

RUNNING AND FLYING

The shape of an animal and the way that animal lives can affect one another. For example, an animal that lives in open spaces must be able to move fast. This is because it has fewer places to hide. So it needs long legs

The modern ostrich (left) and Struthiomimus (right) lived in the same sort of *environment*. They also had similar ways of living. See how alike they are in size and shape.

and a light body. To fly, an animal needs wings and a very light body. Bones are often fused together. This adds strength without weight. An animal that flies must be able to regulate, or control, its body temperature. We know that early birds and pterosaurs could regulate their body temperature from the fossilized remains of feathers and hair.

What works for today's animals worked in the past, too. Scientists can look at an animal's fossilized skeleton. They can tell from its structure what it could do. Then they can tell how it lived.

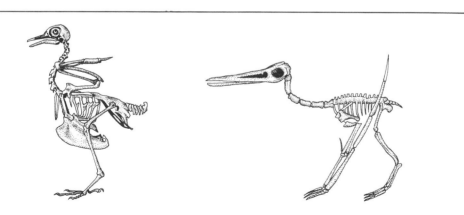

These skeletons are of a pigeon (left) and Pterodactylus (right). Both show front legs that have developed into wings. They have lightly built bodies with many hollow bones.

The dolphin (1), shark (2), and ichthyosaur (3) all have streamlined bodies and a fin or fluke at the tail. They all have fins on each side and on their backs. They all eat fish and have the same lifestyle.

SWIMMING AND BURROWING

The vertebrates of the sea evolved to fit that environment. Their shape shows this.

They had streamlined bodies to help them move through the water. They had fins to steady themselves and to change direction. They had teeth for eating other sea animals. Today's fish are built the same way.

Burrowing animals evolved along the same lines as sea animals. They had a streamlined body for moving through soil or sand.

They moved along by wiggling legs shaped like paddles. Their jaws had small teeth for eating other small animals.

Moles (left) and skinks (right) are burrowing animals. They have streamlined bodies for pushing through the soil.

SCIENTISTS STUDY THE DINOSAURS

In the 1820s Gideon and Mary Mantell found the teeth and bones of the dinosaur Iguanodon. Dr. Mantell put the teeth and bones together. Then he used his knowledge and his imagination, and he restored the animal. It looked like a large lizard. Statues of his Iguanodon are still in England today.

In 1878, 31 complete skeletons of Iguanodon were found in a coal mine in Belgium. Scientists now learned that the animal walked on its hind legs. They also learned that it had a small head and that its bony spike belonged on its thumb and not on its nose. Scientists made new models of Iguanodon.

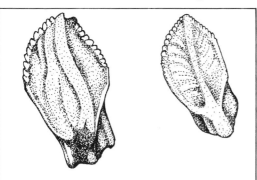

In the 1970s, some scientists suggested that dinosaurs were *warm-blooded*, like mammals and birds today. This led to pictures like the one below. Here, the Iguanodon races like an ostrich of today.

These teeth (above) were the first remains of Iguanodon to be discovered. Dr. Mantell thought the animal walked on all fours, like a huge lizard (below).

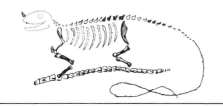

Even today, scientists are finding out new things about these extinct animals. For example, they now think Iguanodon had cheek pouches. New discoveries are being made all the time. No *restoration* is final.

Most modern restorations show Iguanodon this way. Here we see a peaceful-looking animal on its hind legs, eating leaves off a tree.

19

RECONSTRUCTIONS
AND RESTORATIONS

A mounted skeleton is called a *reconstruction*. A restoration shows what the whole animal might have looked like. It may be a painting or a sculpture. Or it might be a photograph.

A restoration starts with a reconstruction. Scientists put together what bones they have. As soon as they find a bone, they make a plaster jacket for it. They do this before they move the bone. Bones are very fragile, and they might break.

Helping paleontologists:
Sometimes, but not very often, fossil skeletons are found in complete form (top).

Sometimes, details like tendons (middle) show that a tail was not flexible.

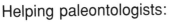

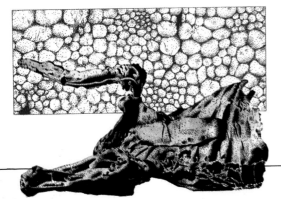

Sometimes, if an animal had been buried quickly, its skin may have been fossilized (bottom).

Paleontologists must figure out how missing bones might be shaped. They look at related animals from the same time.

Paleontologists also look at bones to see how muscles would be attached. They look at how the bones were joined together. This helps them tell if a tail had been stiff or flexible.

Paleontologists also must decide on the color and texture of the skin. Like animals today, large animals may have been darker. Small animals were probably bright.

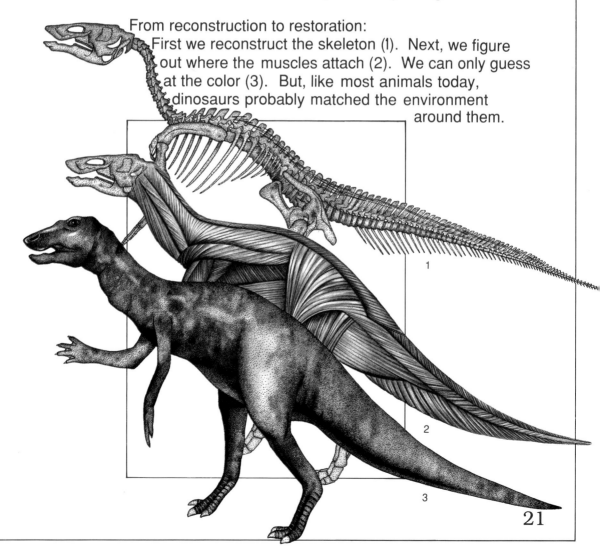

From reconstruction to restoration: First we reconstruct the skeleton (1). Next, we figure out where the muscles attach (2). We can only guess at the color (3). But, like most animals today, dinosaurs probably matched the environment around them.

A MUSEUM RESTORATION

1. Paleontologists make a miniature model.

2. A plywood frame is built. It is covered with wire, then with clay.

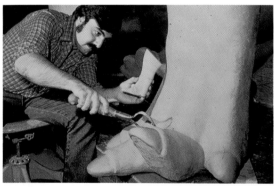

3. The clay is molded to show muscles and skin textures.

4. A mold of hemp and plaster is made over the model. The mold is cut into sections and sent to a caster. The caster makes fiberglass sections out of the mold.

5. Finally the model is painted and put in its habitat group. Here people see the animal with other animals and plants of its time and place.

6. The finished product! Here, Tyrannosaurus Rex feeds on Triceratops as a group of Dromaeosaurus watch. Struthiomimus appears on the painted backdrop.

A PHOTOGRAPHIC RESTORATION

1

2

3

1. Jane Burton positions a model of Styracosaurus in front of the backdrop.

2. She adjusts the glass panels of the backdrop before taking the photographs.

3. The finished picture: a thundering Styracosaurus herd.

THE DISCOVERIES

Since they began looking at rocks, people have known about fossils. They didn't always know what fossils were, though. Some thought fossils were jokes played on them by the gods.

By the mid 1800s, people knew dinosaurs had lived on the Earth. British paleontologists named them *Dinosauria*. This means "terrible reptiles."

In America, two paleontologists began to look for dinosaurs. Their names were Othniel Charles Marsh and Edward Drinker Cope. They were bitter rivals and they were rich. Each one hired large teams to search the US for dinosaur remains. Marsh's teams discovered 80 new species of dinosaur. Cope's found 56 new species.

Othniel Charles Marsh (1831-1899) found many dinosaur remains. He was also a paleontology teacher.

In 1910, the search moved to Canada. The Red Deer River fossil site had been found in Alberta. Between 1909 and 1929, British and German teams found dinosaurs in South Africa and Tanzania.

Since the 1940s, Soviet teams have found big dinosaur graveyards in Mongolia. There have also been finds in China, Australia, and South America in the 20th century.

Dinosaur remains have been found on every continent. They show us much about early animal and plant life. They also give us clues about how the continents once fit together.

Edward Drinker Cope (1840-1897) also led many dinosaur hunts. He and Marsh were rivals.

Since 1960, many discoveries have been made in North America. Paleontologists have unearthed new types of fossil reptiles. Other studies have shown more about how these reptiles lived. Scientists are still studying one problem that they have wondered about since dinsoaurs were first discovered: Why did they disappear?

In the early days, some scientists suggested that great floods or volcanoes killed them all. Later opinions were

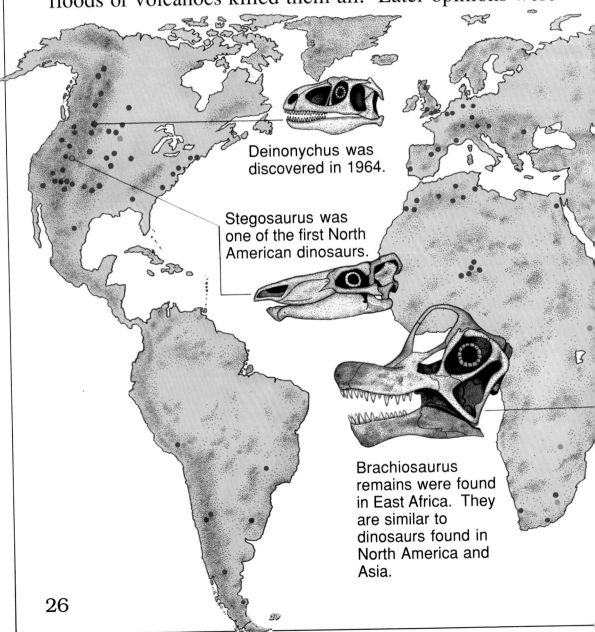

Deinonychus was discovered in 1964.

Stegosaurus was one of the first North American dinosaurs.

Brachiosaurus remains were found in East Africa. They are similar to dinosaurs found in North America and Asia.

that they died out gradually as the plant life and climate changed.

Today, many scientists think a huge meteor strike (seven miles, or 11 km, across) killed the dinosaurs. They say that a meteor strike would have stirred up great clouds of dust. The dust would have blocked out the sun's light for several years, killing the plant life and starving the dinosaurs.

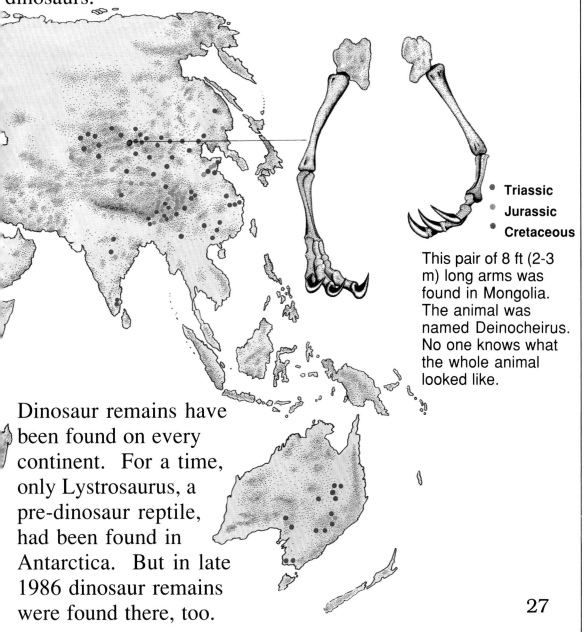

- Triassic
- Jurassic
- Cretaceous

This pair of 8 ft (2-3 m) long arms was found in Mongolia. The animal was named Deinocheirus. No one knows what the whole animal looked like.

Dinosaur remains have been found on every continent. For a time, only Lystrosaurus, a pre-dinosaur reptile, had been found in Antarctica. But in late 1986 dinosaur remains were found there, too.

Fun Facts About Dinosaurs

1. Mary Anning lived from 1799 to 1847. She discovered the first specimen of ichthyosaur in 1811, when she was 12 years old. She discovered the first specimen of plesiosaur in 1824 and the first pterosaur in 1828.

2. In 1878, the skeletons of 31 Iguanodons were discovered during a coal mining excavation in Belgium. It seems that the whole herd had fallen into a ravine and become stuck in a coal swamp. They wound up 1,057 ft (322 m) below the surface of the ground.

3. Edward Drinker Cope wrote his first scientific paper when he was six.

4. From tracks, scientists can tell how a dinosaur moved. Narrow tracks show that the dinosuar walked erect. Long tracks show that the dinosaur could run.

5. There are over 340 known *genera* of dinosaurs. Scientists believe there are more waiting to be discovered.

6. In August, 1966, 2,000 fossil dinosaur tracks were discovered in Rocky Hill, Connecticut. Fifteen hundred of them have been reburied for preservation. You can see the remaining 500, which are sheltered by a geodesic dome. The exact type of dinosaur has not yet been identified. It is probably from the early Jurassic period. It is thought to be related to Dilothosaurus, whose remains have been found in Arizona. The fossil site is now called Dinosaur State Park.

7. Here are some animals that appeared during the Age of Dinosaurs. They are still here today:

turtles — late Triassic period
crocodiles — late Triassic period
sharks (pre-sharks) — Carboniferous period
skates and rays — upper Cretaceous period

8. The animals that we call dinosaurs are actually two subgroups of the group called Archosauria. These two subgroups are Ornithischia, which means "bird-hipped," and Saurischia, which means "lizard-hipped." Both groups include some dinosaurs that walked on two feet and some that walked on four feet. Both groups also include meat-eaters and plant-eaters. The division of dinosaurs into Ornithischia or Saurischia is based on the types of pelvis or hips they have.

More Books About Dinosaurs

Here are some more books about dinosaurs and other animals of their time. If you see any books you would like to read, see if your bookstore or library has them.

All New Dinosaurs and Their Friends from the Great Recent Discoveries. Long & Welles (Bellerphon)
Did Comets Kill the Dinosaurs? Asimov (Gareth Stevens)
Digging up Dinosaurs. Aliki (Harper & Row)

Where to See the Dinosaurs

Fossils, reconstructions, and restorations of dinosaurs and other prehistoric animals are in museums all over the world. Here are some places where you can see them in the United States and Canada.

Zoological Gardens
Calgary, Alberta

Provincial Museum of Alberta
Edmonton, Alberta

Los Angeles County Museum of Natural History
Los Angeles, California

Junior Museum
San Francisco, California

Denver Museum of Natural History
Denver, Colorado

Peabody Museum of Natural History
New Haven, Connecticut

Dinosaur State Park
Rocky Hill, Connecticut

National Museum of Natural History
Washington, D. C.

Field Museum of Natural History
Chicago, Illinois

Science Museum of Minnesota
St. Paul, Minnesota

Museum of the Rockies Bozeman, Montana	Academy of Natural Sciences Philadelphia, Pennsylvania
New Mexico Natural History Museum Albuquerque, New Mexico	Carnegie Museum of Natural History Pittsburgh, Pennsylvania
American Museum of Natural History New York	Houston Museum of Natural Science Houston, Texas
North Carolina Museum Durham, North Carolina	Dinosaur National Monument Jensen, Utah
Stovall Museum Norman, Oklahoma	Utah Museum of Natural History Salt Lake City, Utah
National Museum of Natural Sciences Ottawa, Ontario	Milwaukee Public Museum Milwaukee, Wisconsin
Royal Ontario Museum Toronto, Ontario	W. H. Reed Museum Laramie, Wyoming

New Words

Here are some new words from *Hunting the Dinosaurs and Other Prehistoric Animals*. They appear for the first time in the text in *italics,* just as they appear here.

adapted ....changed to fit new needs

amphibians ....one of the groups of vertebrates, or animals with backbones. Amphibians are cold-blooded, and their skin is smooth.

cold-blooded ....an animal unable to control its body temperature

colonizing ....settling in a group

coniferous (con-IF-er-us)....cone-bearing trees, usually evergreens

continents ....the major land masses of the earth, like North and South America

environment ....the natural home of any plant or animal

evolved..developed by adapting and changing to suit changing environments

extinct ....died out

fossils (fossilized)....................the remains or traces of a plant or animal

genera ....plural of *genus*. A group of closely related species of plants or animals

habitat group ....a display that shows an animal with other animals and plants in a natural landscape

mammal ....one of the groups of vertebrates, or animals with a backbone. Mammals have live babies and nurse their young. Cats, whales, horses, and human beings are mammals.

paleobotany
(pay-lee-o-BOT-an-ee).........the study of plant fossils

paleogeography
(pay-lee-o-gee-OG-rah-fee).the study of the history of the Earth

paleontologists
(pay-lee-on-TOL-o-gists)....scientists who study fossils

reconstruction ....a mounted skeleton of an animal using available fossilized remains

reptile(s) ....an animal that lays its eggs encased in shells on land. Reptiles have horny skin or scales. They are cold-blooded. Lizards, snakes, and crocodiles are reptiles.

restoration ....a portrayal of what an entire animal looked like in life; may be a painting, a sculpture, or even a photographic presentation

structure ....how the parts of something are put together or arranged to form a whole

vertebrates ....animals with a backbone

warm-blooded ....an animal able to control its body temperature

Index and Pronunciation Guide

Archosauria (ark-o-SAW-ree-ah), 29
archosaurs (ARK-o-sawrs), 12, 29

birds, early, 14-15
Brachiosaurus
    (brack-ee-o-SAW-rus), 26

crocodiles (CROC-o-diles), 12, 28

Deinocheirus
    (di-NO-keer-us), 27
Deinonychus (di-NONNI-kus), 26
Dilothosaurus
    (di-LO-tho-SAW-rus), 28
dinosaur, 6, 11, 12-13, 18, 19, 21,
    24-25, 26-27, 28-29
Dinosauria, 24
dolphin, 16
Dromaeosaurus
    (DRO-me-o-SAW-rus), 22

Euparkeria
    (u-par-CARE-ee-ah), 12

fish, 10-11, 16-17
fossils, 6, 8, 15, 20, 24-25

humans, 10-11

ichthyosaur
    (ICK-thee-o-sawr), 16, 28
Iguanodon
    (ig-WAH-no-don), 18-19, 28

lizards, 12, 18
Lystrosaurus (lis-tro-SAW-rus), 27

mammals, 11, 18
moles, 17

Ornithischia ("bird-hipped")
    (or-nih-THISH-ee-ah), 12-13, 29
ostrich, 14, 18

paleontologists, 6, 20-23, 24-25, 26
pigeon, 15
plesiosaur (PLEE-zee-o-sawr), 28
psilophytes (SI-lo-fites), 8
Pterodactylus
    (ter-o-DAC-teh-lus), 15
pterosaurs
    (TER-o-sawrs), 14-15, 28-29

rays, 28
reptiles, 11, 12-13, 24, 26, 27

Saurischia ("lizard-hipped")
    (saw-RISH-ee-ah), 12-13, 29
shark, 16, 28
single-celled animals, 10-11
skates, 28
skinks, 17
snakes, 12
Stegosaurus
    (STEG-o-SAW-rus), 26
Struthiomimus
    (stroo-thee-o-MI-mus), 14, 22
Styracosaurus
    (sty-RACK-o-SAW-rus), 23

thecodont (THEE-co-dont), 12
tortoises (TOR-tiss-es), 12
Triceratops
    (try-SARA-tops), 22
tuatara, 12
turtles, 12, 28
Tyrannosaurus Rex
    (ty-RAN-o-SAW-rus rex), 22

Note: The use of a capital letter for an animal's name means that it is a specific *type*, or *genus*, of animal—like a Stegosaurus or Tyrannosaurus. The use of a lower case, or small, letter means that it is a member of a larger *group* of animals—like ichthyosaurs or crocodiles.